SATYR

SATYR

CLIFF FORSHAW

All rights reserved. No part of this work covered by the copyright herein may be reproduced or used in any means – graphic, electronic, or mechanical, including copying, recording, taping, or information storage and retrieval systems – without written permission of the publisher.

Printed by imprintdigital
Upton Pyne, Exeter
www.digital.imprint.co.uk

Typesetting and cover design by narrator
www.narrator.me.uk
info@narrator.me.uk
033 022 300 39

Published by Shoestring Press
19 Devonshire Avenue, Beeston, Nottingham, NG9 1BS
(0115) 925 1827
www.shoestringpress.co.uk

First published 2017
© Copyright: Cliff Forshaw
© Images copyright (including front cover): Cliff Forshaw

The moral right of the author has been asserted.

ISBN 978-1-910323-85-4

ACKNOWLEDGMENTS

Earlier versions of parts of these poems appeared in: *Sketches, Dispatches, Hull Tales and Ballads* (Kingston Press, Hull City Council 2012); *The Canting Academy: Responses by Contemporary Poets to a 16th Century Rogues' Lexicon*, ed. David Annwn (ISPress, Sheffield 2008).

All illustrations by Cliff Forshaw.

For Stephen Clucas, excellent teacher and friend, who introduced me to John Marston and his psychopathic Malcontent Satyrist alter ego W. Kinsayder, and helped me greatly on the road from London to Oxford.

*An Angelic Conversation or Psychical Curiosity Transcribed,
which the Author hopes may be of passing Interest to
Alienists, Etymologists and the Like.*

SATYR

In the Renaissance, an etymological confusion connected satire with classical satyrs as certain writers adopted the persona of a savage malcontent.

"[Satire] is very railing, onely ordained to rebuke vice… The Satires had their names of uplandysshe Goddes, that were rude, lascivious and wanton of behaviour."
— Thomas Langley (1570)

"It is not for euerybody to relish a true and naturall Satyr, being of itselfe besides the natiue bitternes and tartness of particuliers, both hard of conceipt, and harsh of stile, and therefore cannot but be vnpleasing both to the vnskilfull, and ouer Musicall eare."
— Joseph Hall (1599)

"Difficile est satyram non scribere"
— Juvenal

"Let Custards quake, my rage must freely runne"
— W.Kinsayder (a.k.a. John Marston) *The Scourge of Villainie* (1598)

In a moment, in the twinkling of an eye, at the last trump: for the trumpet shall sound, and the dead shall be raised incorruptible, and we shall be changed.
— King James Bible 1 Corinthians 15:52

Dr Quodlibet, Renowned Psychopomp, en Séance, makes the Acquaintance of Divers Others, from Whence we know not (perhaps some Ancient Pagan Realm?) and transcribes their strange Enochian.

Coming in. Coming in...

See them in their bold effrontery,
these *Meteors, Gloworms, Rats of Nilus*,
with their lingos, winks and elbow nudgery:

slinking through this city without a skin,
jiving greasy guns. O the blatant cockery
of these *Nightshades, Chameleons*, and *Apparitions*.

Hoodie-boyos, chaveris, adipose hussies with their open purses,
the *Scally* jazzing with Blunt and Redtop
till beer o'clock and time to slop

stilton tattoos along brass-top or naugahyde;
his proud shout drilling the barkeep's dischuffed dial,
unenrapt without pourboire or promises thereof;

then on, with Latvio-Lithuo-Sengali-Ivorian cab-driver
(PhD in Astronomy, Agronomy, Homiletics or Dark Matter).
Drop him the change from one lonely deepsea diver,

then on, always on,
to badly-packed kebabs or bacon banjos.
Takeaway. Takeaway. Graze on the hoof.

Another blunt, a toot, another blow on the bugle:
hoovering the kermit for the last of the Devil's dandruff
– confuzzled in the karzy, gone completely hatstand.

Carking it on the big white telephone to God,
in technicolour prayer. Thou art translated
to some new Beast. Behold the Bog Ostrich!

O Shapes transform'd to Bodies straunge!
O godly Creatures! O brave new World!
My new-found Land! My Ingerland!

*

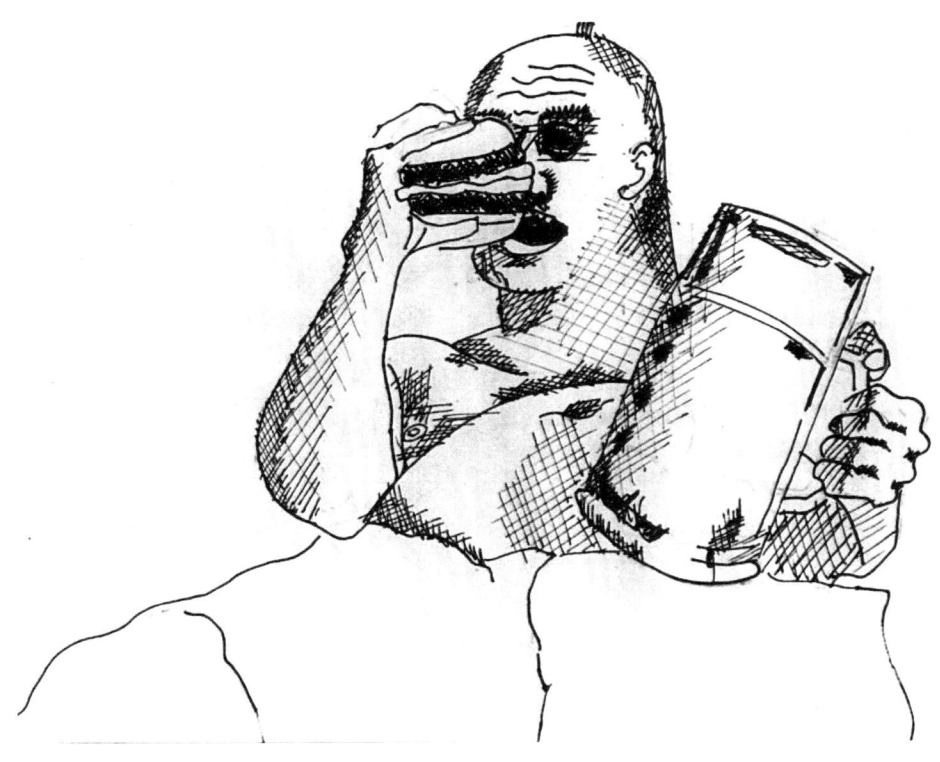

An Aside in which the Satyr Discourses upon his Ancient Art

Both incense and the human reek
Are best described in Attic Greek.
Autre temps, autre moeurs,
Those ancients knew just how to curse.

But way back then in Classic Times,
They thought it vulgar to use rhymes.
However, this barbaric Tongue
Has dealt us Spades for shovelling Dung.

With Rasp & Scratch it hardly sings,
But bang it hard and Iron rings.
As much as any metric choice,
"Iambic" meant a tone of voice:

An ancient and sarcastic focus
(Since Hipponax and Archilochus).
From IAPTO: "to assail",
Iambicists lampooned and railed.

Between their tragedies, the Greeks
(When Oedipus seemed to last for weeks)
Liked a little vulgar farce:
Carry On Tits, a farting Arse.

We Satyrs mocked the tragic Fates:
Silenus, myself, a dozen mates.
Priapus did a magic trick
And comic stand-up with his dick.

The audience, easily amused,
Kept our goat-skins filled with booze.
No one dared to get their coat,
They knew that that would get our goat.

Uz Satyrs can be really snide
– oh yes, we have our nasty side.
You see that when we've had a skinful,
We take delight in being sinful.
    Likewise Man, when he gets pissed,
    becomes a snarling Satyrist.

*

Ingerland: foreskin of a Friday night.
DJ, eyes worn by distance, smoke,
eavesdrops the future down the bone,
thumbs the next track into the stripper's zip,
wastes imported vinyl on the drongos of this Dead Zone.

Thud and blunder from the back-room.
Click of a black rolls the last pony into the pocket.
You trouser what you can of the chink,
stand your wingman a chaser, and one for the bludger,
stuff a brown lizzie in the burly-gurlie's biscuit.

Out into the bladdered, the Filth with their hoolivan,
faces like bulldogs licking piss off a nettle.
Everyone, everywhere's angstin or bustin for knuckle.
And it's a jive life. *Jive life. Jive life.*

*

Outside in bum-fuck Egypt, garyboys burn rubber,
gunning kevved-up GTs, twerking twocked Zondas.
You go down manors icky with gum and spilt claret,
rug like a pub floor that sticks to the sole.

Past glassy piss-factories, vitrines of vertical drinkers,
smokers and vapers, smartphones flipped, juggled on the flop,
the jig and jag, the jokey rib-punch, joshing on the step,
the middling men paunching untucked shirts.

Past face-aches, blue-rinsers, tranked Neds and jellied Nellies,
the liggers, lounge-lizards, the bilious prannets with previous;
over the vom, coffin-dodgers, pavement pizzas.

Past Halal Taxi, Polski Smak (Scag? S&M? Happy-slappers?).
Through carparks, ruinous estates, urinous underpasses
carpeted by bozos, piss-pants and crusty-white rastas.

*

Up there the bunker: rachitic saplings on a raw-estate,
the boarded-up shops, bars on barwindows. Inside asboids,
pickled eggs, pork scratchings, Britain's Hardest Landlord,

ripped leatherette and coughed-up stuffing.
It's all argument, argot and grot; booze, palaver and pants.
Give me your piss-poor, your pilchards, your pillocks.

Think back to the old blokes, the smoky Snug, the snecklifter;
the art-college year, the one you dropped out for the boozer till 3,
Somali Club afternoons, and back again for early doors.

That urgent note drilling the zinc, ringing out loud
–ah the paintings you'd paint, the poems you'd write! –
as you emptied all your warmth in the singing pissoir.

*

The whore wore a perfume called Slut,
    a short skirt with a meaningful slit:
knackered and knickerless; Aviation Blonde
    by the look of her black box.
The mad joker's eyes, quick sticks
    from jack and danny to her rack.
Body off Baywatch, face off Crimewatch.
    The rest were all rammy, radged real bad.
You'd of ralphed or prayed to an Old Testament God,
    to jimmy you out, drop you back on your tod
in the pustular choky of your cold-water sock.

*

Here come the Silicon Valley girls, well not quite:
their figures lardily imprecise, but they got chips all right
and corned-beef legs. And beer tits! beer tits!
Muffintops, piercings, builder's crack:
cankles and arsewag and the requisite
cantilevered quondam of cleavage.

Sonnet of the Blazon of the Bloody Big Beauties

O beerbosomed Blowsies, all Brastraps, and Chipsauce;
O Denizens of the Deep-Fry, all Moon-Face and Bling
— I am torn by the Manichean Schism of thy Thong Cheeks.
O Chlamydia, banged up with Arsehats, and Losers;
O Minger sat on your Bahookie down the Boozer;
O lardy lardy Ladies, Tattoos growing into the Sofa,
With skanky Ankle-Biters, sugar high and screeching,
Remote down your Backside, maybe remote from you forever.
Up there the Gob, 'cos she's worth it, the skinny Ho,
All Vogue on the outside and vague on the in.
O Rhadamanth! O Callipygous! O Essex got Talent.
Got Wrap, Surf 'n' Turf. Got Taco, Panini.
Go Supersize with Fries. Go main-course on the side.
O Aphrodite! O lewd Britannia! O Go, Girl, GO!

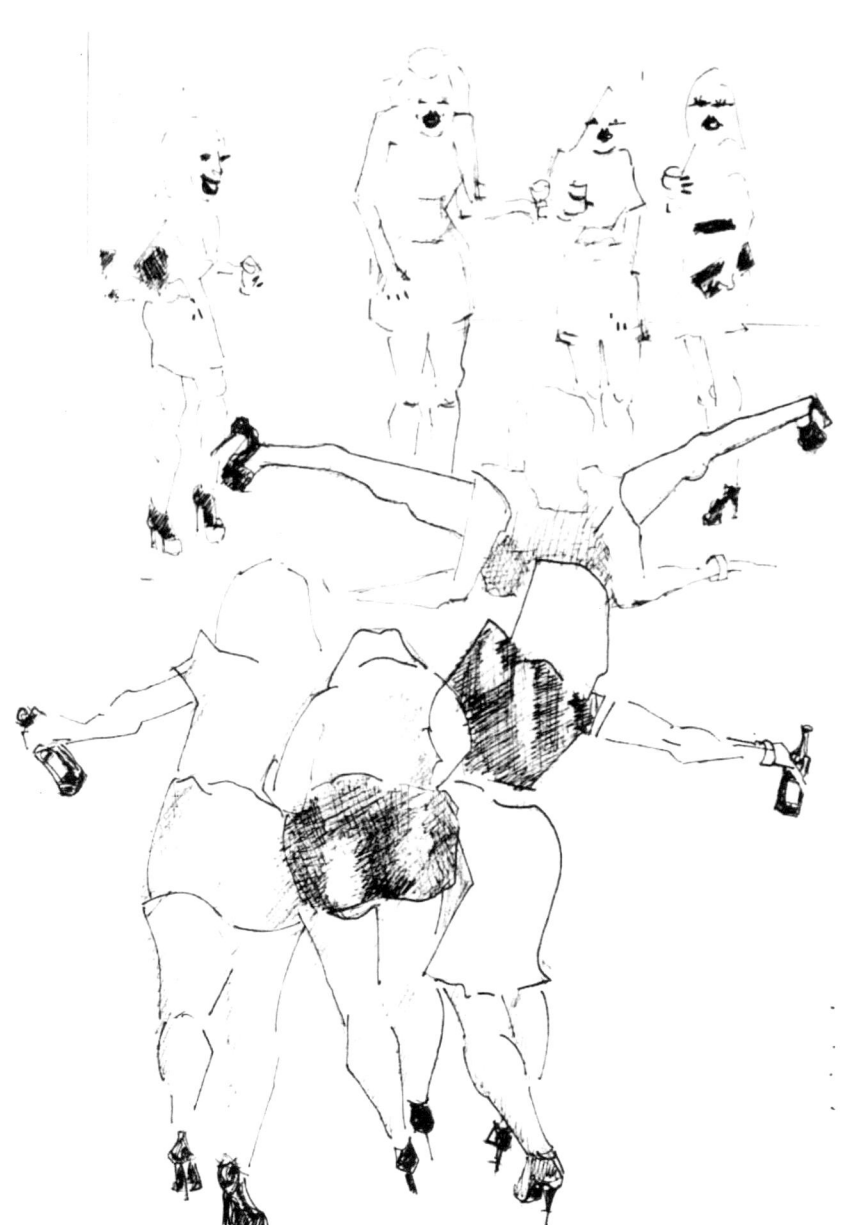

Her Lips are glossed, her Breasts are pert:
Queen Brittany rips off her Skirt.
See Toad-Skin, Warts, Buboes, Scales;
Foul Underparts, a slimy Tail.

Shifting Borders, formal Rape,
Now Nothing keeps within its Shape.
Circe's famous magic Stunt
Turned men to Pigs and made 'em grunt.

Thus deprived of Human Will,
They frolicked, happy in the Swill.
But One among these transformed Swine,
Had never felt so pigging fine.

When Circe charmed them back to Men,
He begged to be a Pig again.

*

Good news that Darwin's fittest winner
no longer needs to hunt for dinner.
Man's evolved, no longer brute,
has furry friends who are cuddly, cute.

(Darwinian parasites not fit
to do much more than eat, piss, shit.)
But Man's best friends must now survive
the beauty contest that goes out live.

The Master's face is here reflected
by beasts invented or subjected.
In his image what he's created:
denatured, timid, enslaved, castrated;

pets that worship or things that yield
– drugged and pregnant – in a field
if they're lucky, a box if not,
bio-engineered for the pot.

Cold pastoral – so clever and so big:
it's cow eat cow and pig eat pig.
To turn a buck from animals,
you've turned them into cannibals.

> *You hate the wild, you fear what rages,*
> *you like your beasts pent up in cages.*
>
> *And what's still red in tooth and claw?*
> *– Not manicured nails on the lapdog's paw*
> *but (O lesser breeds without the law!)*
> *the gangsta's pit-bull chain-saw jaw.*

O Sister Moon, Big Brother Sun,
Man and animal live as one.
Be meek. Obey. Or you'll be beaten.
Your brothers are bred just to be eaten.

O Brother Wolf, O Sister Horse,
This is how it works of course:
Steal what you want; kill what you can,
For Man's a Wolf to his fellow Man.

*

The Satyr's Goat Song

The Lord is Your Shepherd, that's OK for sheep,
    but, half-man and half-beast, a Greek god in my sleep,
cocksure and awkward, obscene and not herd,
    I'm Dick the Shit, I'm Richard the Turd.
The guy who put the man in Manic,
    the god who gave his name to Panic,
the mounting goat who tupped the flock,
    King Billy Bollocks with his red-hot cock.
Horny and rampant, a battering ram,
    I screwed the Ewe, lay down with the Lamb.
I'm the King of Misrule, the Master of Revels,
    the original horned and cloven-foot Devil.
From my horns right down to each hoof I'm split:
    I see the bad in others because I know I'm shit.
And I know the lust inside of you,
    because it boils inside me too.
And you're no stranger to my anger:
    when did you ever look back in languor?
I have felt your every grudge,
    that's why I'm fit to be your judge.
To triangulate the human race,
    the apex rises from what's base.
The *hypocrite lecteur* (wrote Baudelaire)
    is both my semblance and my *frère*.
And if I am a hypocrite,
    part-time moralist and full-time shit,
in that I am your twin, your mirror, too,
    and what you see in me – just look,
(just look within) – is YOU!

*

Mondays we wuz bug hunting
down near the cemetery,
buzzing the bonies, no need
of chivvin the pigeons,
but a little dip and dab.
Was near a deadlurk, when…

*

You hear the little twoats dunting the street,
rotwiled by schnauzers nicknocked Asbo and Kewl,
wonder, in a vaguely Mallarméan way,
how to purify the dialect of this tribe.
But we're rolling out and heading up,
counting zero-sum and mission creep;
taking a reality check and going forward
One Hundred and Twenty Percent Iconic.
How quick your rug-rat's become a little twagger,
got a Desmond from the Academy of Cant.

*

Your future now sulks through its teens.
Hidden behind the glowing screens,
they celebrate a new Communion:
a breadless, wineless, bodiless Union.
Webbed life slips through the holey Net
– they think they surf, but they don't get wet.

*

all coming in, coming in, coming in… can't keep those voices out of my head

zero hours, cashback, Uber	work-life balance, payday Wonga
knowledge nomads, sofa-surfers	creative migrants, foreign workers
networking, light-touch regulation	anywhere/anytime, wealth creation
Facebook, facetime, one-on-one	online identity, always on
blurring boundaries, internet use	social media, trolls, abuse
privately-funded, PPI	norovirus, e coli
Powerpoint, Krispy Kreme	donut town, government scheme
CPD, BOGOF, quality metrics	belly-buster, all day Brexit
algorithms, geometric vectors	data culture across the sector
integrated software platforms	patent-pending GM life-forms
health care professional, download app	social worker, benefit cap
health insurance, two for one	floppy-haired telly-don
navigating stresses, managed decline	legal highs and a fine white line
economies of scale, competitive edge	cut-backs, hedge fund

wedge, wedge, wedge

waste disposal, municipal dump	Cameron, Johnson, Farage, Trump
health insurance, be prepared	geriatric homes, no one cared
extraordinary rendition, going for a song	deprive this banker of his gong!
scrolling down through Tinder, Grindr	profile of President Putin's minder
key-stage, benchmarks, peer review	What the fuck's it to do with you?
kitemark, feedback, nickle and dime	bedblocker demographics, sub-prime
The Art of War, a skinny latte	neo-con, fiscal karate
full-time carer, glossy hair	corporate buy-out, questionnaire
black ops, psy-ops, free makeover	asset stripping, new Range Rover

The Satyr Paints a Trinity of Genomic Portraits for Charles Darwin

Artist Marc Quinn has made a "genomic portrait" of Sir John Sulston, a key figure in the development of the analysis of DNA and the definition of the human genome. The geneticist's DNA is encased in a frame which mirrors the observer. Here, 23 couplets represent the 23 pairs of human chromosomes.

1   In the Name of the Father

This kind of portrait's just your name
    with DNA in a metal frame.
You look into the glass and see
    reflected back, both you *and* me.
Long molecules of the human race
    hold mirrors up to the voyeur's face.
From Genesis, here's Revelation:
    Creation's mostly Information.
Magnified, they're twisted crosses:
    X marks the spots of gains and losses.
Each gene projects the trait it means
    upon the human plasma screens.
State-of-the-art, sharp resolution
    in byte-sized, digital, *Evolution*.
Conceptually, now re-creation's
    a pigment of the imagination.
Skin-deep, cosmetic – paint betrays
    the *made-up* thing that it portrays.
The stuff that paints eyes brown or blue
    's no medium for catching you.
The family portrait's now replaced,
    ID's conceived to be *defaced*.
Your skin's tattooed, your hair is dyed,
    both painting and the camera lied.
Your nose is trimmed, your breasts augmented,
    your eyes in contacts look demented.
With sculpted cheeks and capped white teeth,
    God only knows what lies beneath.
Not just the skull beneath the skin,
    we want to see what's deep within.

We want to see what's really dark
    – survival earned through each black mark.
Now, paint-by-numbers DNA
    with radioactive markers, say,
might, as the Geiger ticked away,
    catch your half-life, hint at decay.
This is the sequence marked down through time
    – those narcissistic couplets rhyme.
But duplication's not so great:
    the verses limp, the genes mutate.
Like chromosomes in twos – your doubles –
    each wriggling pair now looks for trouble.
Each chromosome's a mirrored X,
    which, naturally, goes wrong with sex.
Y is one at such a loss:
    three-legged beast or broken cross?

2 And the Son

X kisses X, or does it lie?
    Twenty-two times, then maybe Y.
This snapshot of your DNA
    can't really catch you here, today.
Genetic stuff is so abundant,
    that most of it can seem redundant.
Point one percent's what makes you *YOU*,
    suspended here in living glue.
You're stuck into prehistory
    along with dinosaurs and me.
Ninety-nine point nine percent
    of your genes are no different
from Hitler's, Stalin's or Pol Pot's.
    To draw yourself, best join the dots.
Dot each "i", but write it small,
    trace the ego to the Fall.
Most genes within the double helix
    are shared with Rover, Mickey, Felix
– not only cuddly, furry friends,
    the snake and fish have shaped our ends.
You share the stuff that sculpts your features
    with a billion loathsome creatures.
And genes that make a frog or toad
    are scanned to form your own barcode.
The genetic code which seals your fate's
    mere digits away from rough primates.
You stand upright, although you limp:
    you're 98% a chimp.
Your kids may lack a shaggy coat,
    but if they're yours they're still half-goat.
Your sister-in-law, you see her now,
    not merely bovine, but true cow.
A chance mutation makes you strong:
    a broken gene that copies wrong.
Relentless pressure's really grim,
    the future of most species dim.
And even those who do survive,

must journey on, no one arrives.
No intervention from the gods
    will save an ape or change the odds.
O Tech-Fix desperate Hi-Hope junkies,
    no God appears to give a monkey's.
Genomic portraits intimate
    the accident of birth that's fate
… and Nazi Nature's Final Solution
    – Oblivion – drives evolution.

3   And the Wholly Ghost

No God creates a brand new species:
    the future teems in bogs and faeces.
No Creator ticks them off His list,
    there is no bio-alchemist.
A zillion misses, then a hit,
    a chance mutation transforms shit.
The whole thing is a sort of Zen:
    can gods exist if there's no men?
It never stops, nothing remains,
    we're tangled up in endless chains.
All change! All change! No time to think.
    Goodbye, you are the weakest link!
Survival of the fittest, sure,
    but then the rules tell us much more.
It's A Knockout! and every round
    grinds the weak into the ground.
It's not so much the fit survive,
    but that the weak aren't left alive.
Then Man stood up and changed the rules:
    he used his brain, invented tools.
He learned to cut his hair and talk,
    to wash his hands and use a fork.
Top Dog sits down to Nature's feast,
    dog's off the menu – he's no beast.
How like a God! So worldly-wise,
    his mission's now to civilize.
But the problem with increased survival
    is that his brother's now his rival.
"Darwinian" as a term now means
    economics more than genes.
If bees evolved producing honey,
    is there a gene for making money?
You're what you drive and what you wear;
    you're what you buy – *Suits you, sir*.
Platinum Amex flashed on a date
    proclaims the new eugenic mate.
The peacock with his fine display,

>the ostentatious way to pay:
both proclaim a sort of health
>– in modern terms, we're talking wealth.
Old bodies, once fit for only worms,
>have cloned their youth and banked their sperms.
Genetic engineering can
>turn frozen rich to Superman.
See Lazarus rising from the body's tomb,
>the lab's the modern virgin womb.

*

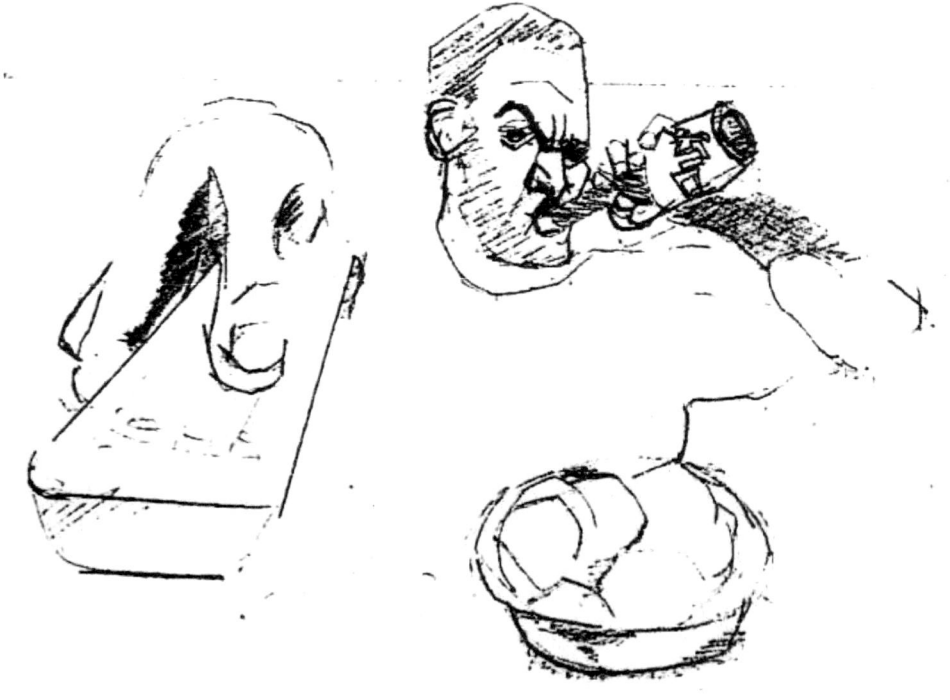

The Satyr Considers the News

Quake guzzle dogs, that live on putrid slime,
Skud from the lashes of my whipcrack rhyme.
Another stinking fog blocks out the sun,
Let Custards quake, my rage must freely runne.

The Last Trump sounds, a mighty Fart.
My reply's this rallentando artillery of Art.
Sniff backed-up Sewers, the spilling Swill
From the shining City upon the Hill.
See how the Rogues fog Facts to Buggery,
Feeding piggish Demagoguery.

Who are these Things? These puffed-up Lizards?
These Wind-Socks, Spindrifts, Focus-Group Wizards?
Mere empty Balloons, pontificating Bubbles,
Arse-Wind blown above the Rubble
Of flattened Nineveh, ruin'd Tyre.

See starving Sidon; feel the Rabble's Breath;
Smell Corruption, Pestilence and Death.
Bring me my Lyre of barbed and tangled Wire
To hymn the Bodies thrown upon the Pyre.

The right-on Right Hon asks Questions for Cash,
Snivels under the Whip or Miss Whiplash,
Snorts Jobs from the Breasts of trafficked Trade,
Cuts deals with Coke and Weapon's Grade…
O we go down, O we go down…

Pluto. Plutocracy. Plutonium. Polonium,
And you're all on your ownium,
Very much on your ownium.

We knew little, but it all went on, I'm sure
– the Lords in puff-up ruffs, ballooning slops.
Milord Walsingham took care of that.
Now we see much more; are wired and seen,
in skin or skankpants, scammed, surveilled by screen.
It's a fair enough cop. Black ops. Black ops,
for the omnipresent Red Tops.

Devices scrolling in every eye,
virtually cradled, digging our digital graves.
The forgotten lexicons for Nature, mates.
Woods and words, all chopped, deleted;
algorithms turn fiends to Friends, destinies to Fate,
the world that was so full now so depleted.

And, here we are, all cabbaged on a corner,
casting nasturtiums on the Big Boys' reps.

> The *Hypocrite* in Ancient Greek
> meant one arraigned before his judges:
> I *know* I'm angry, arrogant, weak,
> prurient, prone to bearing grudges.

> But he who makes a Beast of himself
> gets rid of the fear of being a Man,
> grows goaty shanks, great cloven hooves,
> and hurls his own shit at the fan.
> His eyes like caprine minus signs
> negate all light; he whinges, whines.

I saw: the asset stripper at the stripper's ass,
the Knights of Dollarous Countenance in thrall
to the Machiavells and politickers. I saw it all
as the planet cooked and the forests continued to fall;

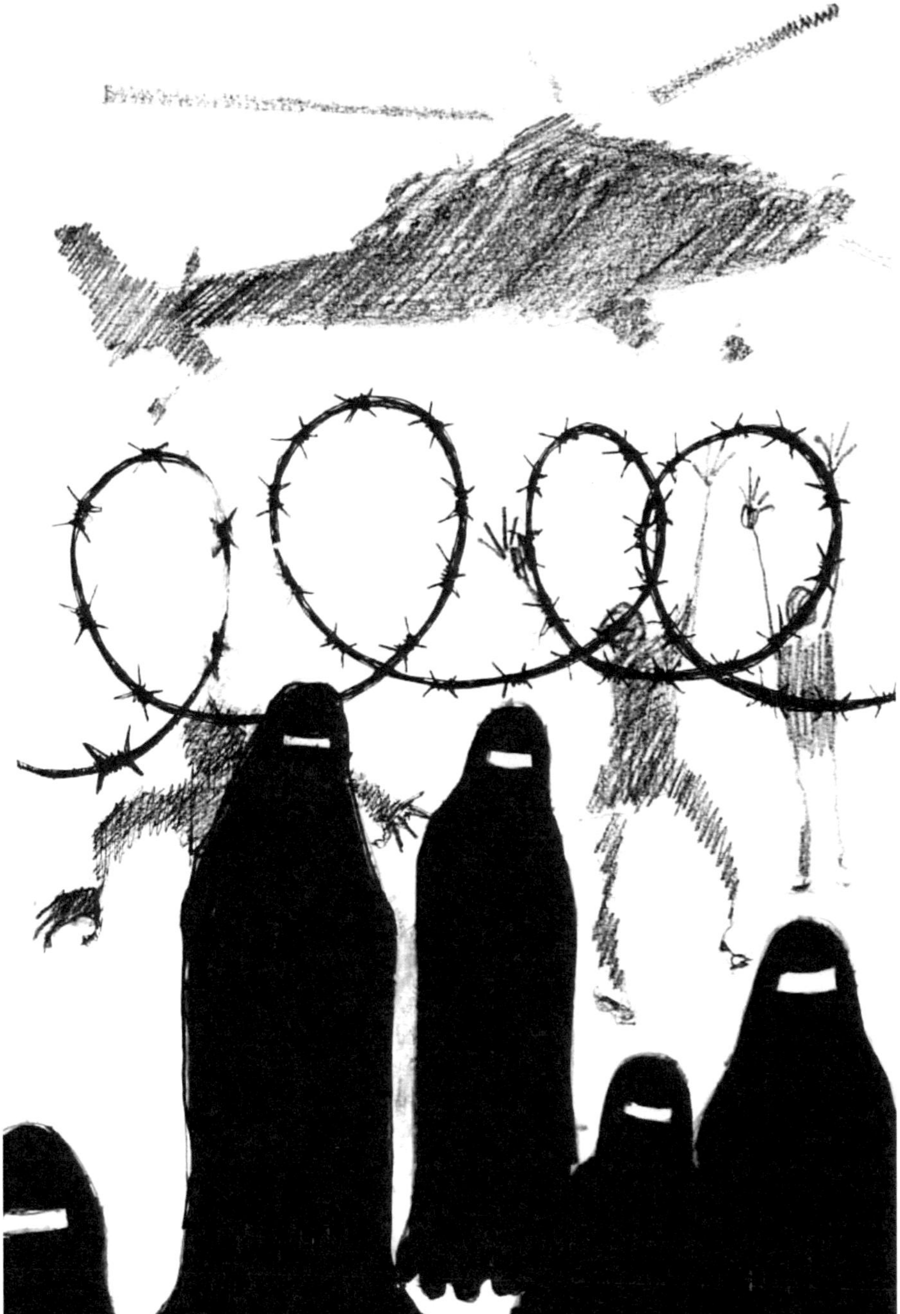

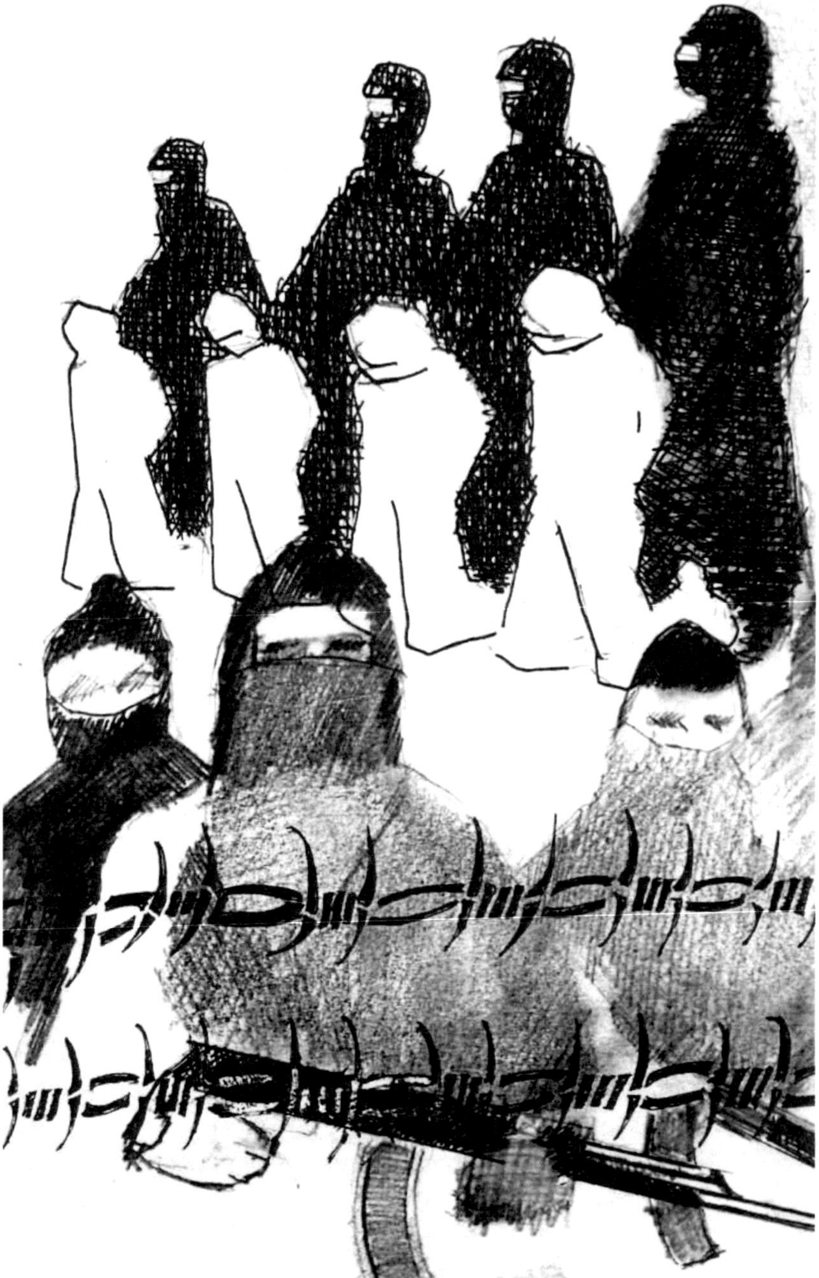

the FTSE, the Nikkei, the Sendai, the Bourse;
I saw it all: the homeless, the stateless, the wounded,
the refugees, and the corpses, of course.

> Bring me my lyre of barbed and tangled wire,
> my barbiton of jangling razor blades.
> Bring me my pen, my ink of poisoned slime,
> to set down my dirty ditty, my putrid rhyme.

*

The headlines drilling the head each day:
'It'll be 52 visits until we can be together again'
A WOMAN who stabbed her fiancé as he slept has been jailed for three years after her partner begged for leniency. Chardonnay Newton, 32, stabbed chef Grigory Pumpkin at their flat in... MARRY ME EVEN THOUGH YOU STABBED ME

A mother who made her children work as slaves after falling under the spell of a fortune teller is facing jail. Mum-of-four Chelsea Brough...

Boy,12, sells porno DVDs from kebab van.

Three children found naked in street while she went for a night out. Tanned, manicured and carrying a designer handbag, this is the mum, 26, who went on a drunken night out leaving her three young children home alone in a filthy house.

Jail for parents who gave *methadone* to son for at least eight months before he died at the age of 23 months... Guinness, 28, and Destiny, 26, did not find their son's body for at least five hours because they were "groggy" and "hungover" after taking drugs and vodka. Both parents wept in the dock. Parents cannot administer methadone like Calpol, said Chief Inspector...

78-year-old grandmother handed interim Asbo for pestering police.

MASS BRAWL Notorious criminal was left unconscious after a gang of hooligans started a mass brawl in a city centre pub. The 40-year-old was celebrating his son's 18th birthday... kicked him repeatedly in the... threw a glass... pulled a knife....

Man loses baby on pub-crawl.

The headlines drilling the head each day:
papers, freesheets, flyers from the takeaway;
kebabbed, pizzaed, burgered JUST EAT!
crisp bags, PET bottles crusting the street.
And here, an invitation, flapping at your feet.

> Due to many requests
> PSYCHIC EVENING & CARVERY
> Renowned Spiritual Medium
> IRIS MARSTON
> WITH SPECIAL GUEST

I found myself at that pub whose entertainment boasted
The Psychic Carvery. Mine Host
introduced the Renowned Spiritual Medium.
The air shimmered above steamed veg, logs of felled beef;
all was greasy tedium.

Was then I felt the starchy spokes, my neck wound round with linen:
slipped the halo that served my head up on a plate.
My apple bobbed, o that old Adam; jacket tightened,
stiffened to a doublet slit with silk;
and I was sharp as a stiletto up from the waist;
below a bludger thickened, swollen, puffed out
those thistledown pants....
below that still the matted shanks.
The curl upon the chin, the snarl of lips,
and the horns now budding through the brow.
And I am up for scut and rutting, I clop
Ram-Alley Billy, ram all who get my goat.

I passed through the lonely, the bereaved piling their plates;
felt no other ghastly guest among stuck hips, shifting teeth;
nothing there that didn't wheeze or dimple the acrylic.

Then I realised it was down to me to do my best.
They were all waiting for a visitation.
It was me who was that Special Guest.

I settled on the psychic, became the side-kick
she'd never had, then clattered my hooves right down the table,
scattered cutlery and platters, the whole shebang to fuckety,
and I was more alive, though dead,
than any who tried to get their head
round what was going on.

And then I realised I was more dead,
more dead than any of the generations who
had failed to take up their bed and walk.
Dead as that steamed veg, that leg of ham,
that log of beef, that hunchbacked turkey.
My skin as dead and rubbery as the thickening gravy.

And all around was insubstantial mist,
incorporeal as that thing I had become.
My hand before me was hung with a veil of flesh,
my eyes x-rayed the crab of bone beneath.
I was a flicker in the cage that ribbed my chest,
my skull a Plato's cave I could not escape.

*

And all I saw, I saw right through: shadow
mated with shadow for seconds, aeons…
But the world blubbered on, its heft inglorious grease.
Huge balloons of fat bounced along the street,
puttered pavements in scootered mobility.

O my Chameleon Muse, lend me your eyes!
I see through all these Shift-Skins and realise
I'm another swivel-eyed reptilian:

Fork-tongued, prurient, angry, mendacious, weak:
Great Nothing of slurry, clothed in knitted meat;
I mirror all we've caged, declawed, debeaked.

You text, don't call. Email, don't go next door.
You Screen the World and all its texture out.
You're everywhere but here. Don't know you're born.
You're Googled maps. Sexting. Smartphone porn.

Once, I thought it had surely come, the hour
To sort the child, the slave, the angel, whore
To their respective fates. All now decays:

We find ourselves confused, minds fogged by din;
Committed to transcendence as never before.
Air darkens, we strain our eyes but only see
The flickers of the fateful circuitry
That we have put our faith, our futures in.

       And I am impotent to purge the snotterie and slime;
       Fade to *Colosses, Mountebancke*s, foul *Apes,*
       The lewde Priapians, and gouty *Humours* of my former time.

*

The Satyr Observes the Hidden Lives of the Ancient and the Wise

There was an old lady who lived in a shoe

China dolls in national dresses,
statuettes of shepherdesses,
complicated glass knick-knacks,
magazine and letter racks...

The heating's up, the room is stuffy;
her world's a slipper, pink and fluffy.
Who says old age should rage, rage, rage,
not shelter now in pastel, beige?

The wicked world outside appals,
she hears it coming through the walls.
The corridor's a ghostly crowd,
her door's a deaf-aid turned up loud.

Peevish voices while she sings.
The freezer beeps, the oven rings.
Now ears are blunted like her eyes,
she hears machines ventriloquise.

These make her feel she's less alone,
(her daughter's voice on the answerphone).
Then the intercom's stentorian crackle
turns postman or nurse to witch's cackle.

From her armchair she can always see
the doorway on CCTV.
She watches all who come and go
channelled through the video.

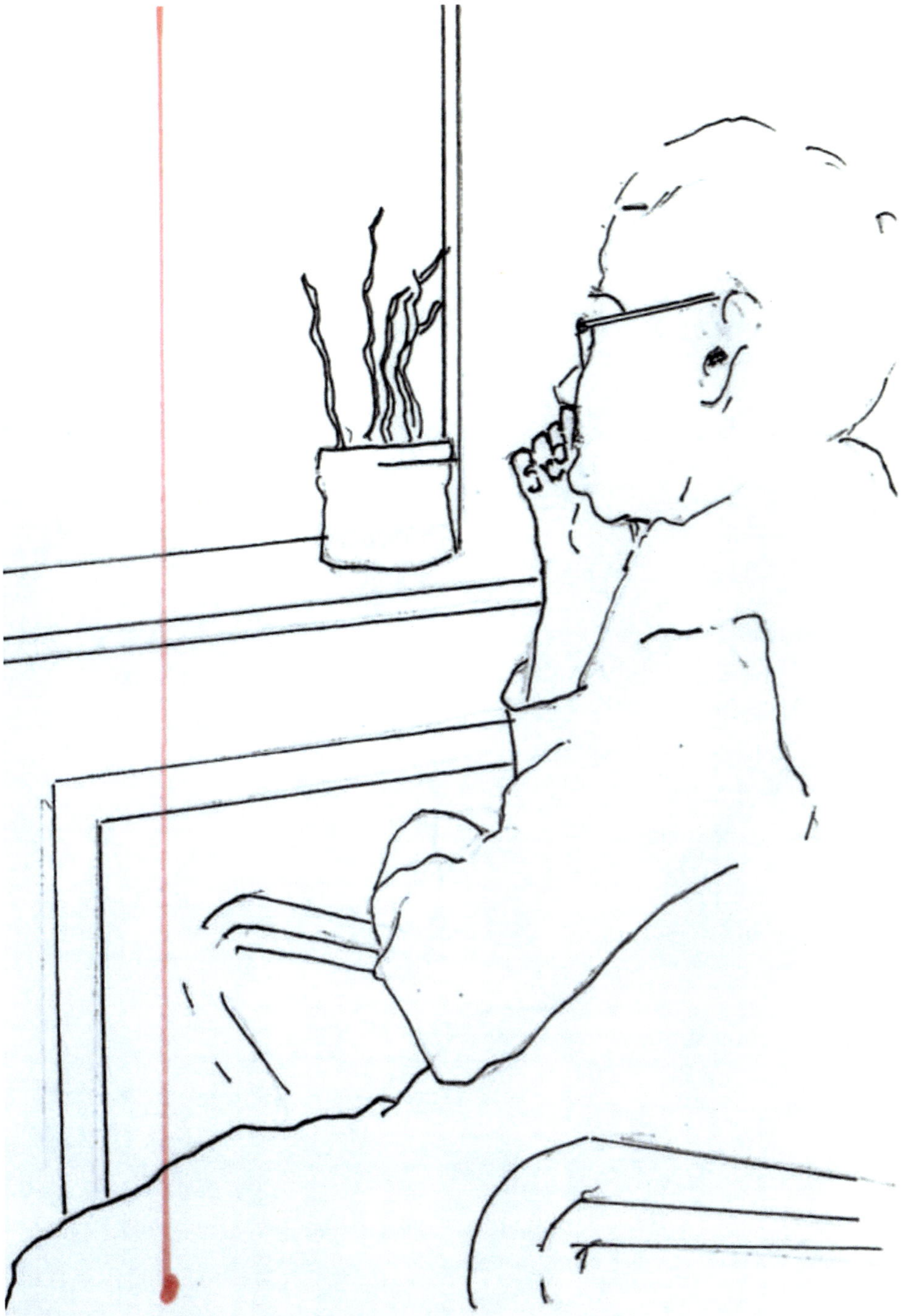

Ancient Goddess of the Gates,
she sees through those for whom she waits.
Visitors ghost bifocal eyes
– grey shades which don't materialise.

A machine she cannot understand:
the remote is trembling in her hand.
Sometimes she thinks she sees her daughter
(a shame the girl had never taught her
to operate this thing she'd bought her).

She dozes, naps, takes forty winks
as digital green numbers blink.
Zeroes stutter, time stands still,
the countdown flashes NIL-NIL-NIL.

Snoozing now on borrowed time,
she scares herself with real-life crime.
Is this No-Man's-Land *Crimewatch* reports
the home for which her husband fought?

    Above the Magicoal's red burn,
    the burnished medals, the tiny urn…

She's had her world, now all has changed:
the outside's lawless, wild, deranged.
All that is solid melts into air;
she prays to God. Is He still there?

Eternal Life, or glowing dreams,
sold with unguents, salves and creams.
Are Heaven, Hell just holy fictions?
Your faith best put in repeat prescriptions?

Petticoated rolls in pink,
a canister to mace the stink
of every memory that haunts
the failing body's secret taunts.

*And if she stumbles, gets sad or bored,
in every room hangs a red ripcord.*

*

The Satyr Bids Quodlibet Adieu: The Maledictor His Valediction

Was chuffed as nuts, felt I really fitted in,
capering in your Beastly Den,
with the upchucking chicklets and chundering men,
the charvers all bobbinsed and bladdered and biffed,
the chavtastically cabbaged, the chang-chonged and spliffed.

I borrowed your body, hitched a ride on your bones.
The clatter of my hooves meant you were never alone.
My shaggy loins forked into your shins.
My horny buds poked through your skin.

 And I have been your true amigo,
 no one closer, your alter ego.
 But now it's time to be out of here.
 Got to get my arse in gear.

I say goodbye to all of you:
the Dorises, douche-bags, dumbnuts, and dorks,
the fugly, feckers, faffers, farts,
the gadgies, gagas, gaffers, geeks,
the gobsmacked, gobshites, jakeys in Jeeps,
the pickled, piddling, porkers with peng,
the snockered, snitchers, spods who can't sing,
twannocks talking trousers twenty-four seven,
the twonks on the womble, the Craigs and the Kevins.

 I take my leave of your sad bones,
 tattoos, piercings, 'roid rage, iPhones,
 Charlie, acid, skunk, skank, weed
 (when it comes to the Pharmakon, I think I'm up to speed).

Farewell to rabbits, dildonics, all slatterns of electricity,
all box-set DVDs featuring epic psychopathy and furious fatalities,
and all the other diversions from your inevitable mortality.

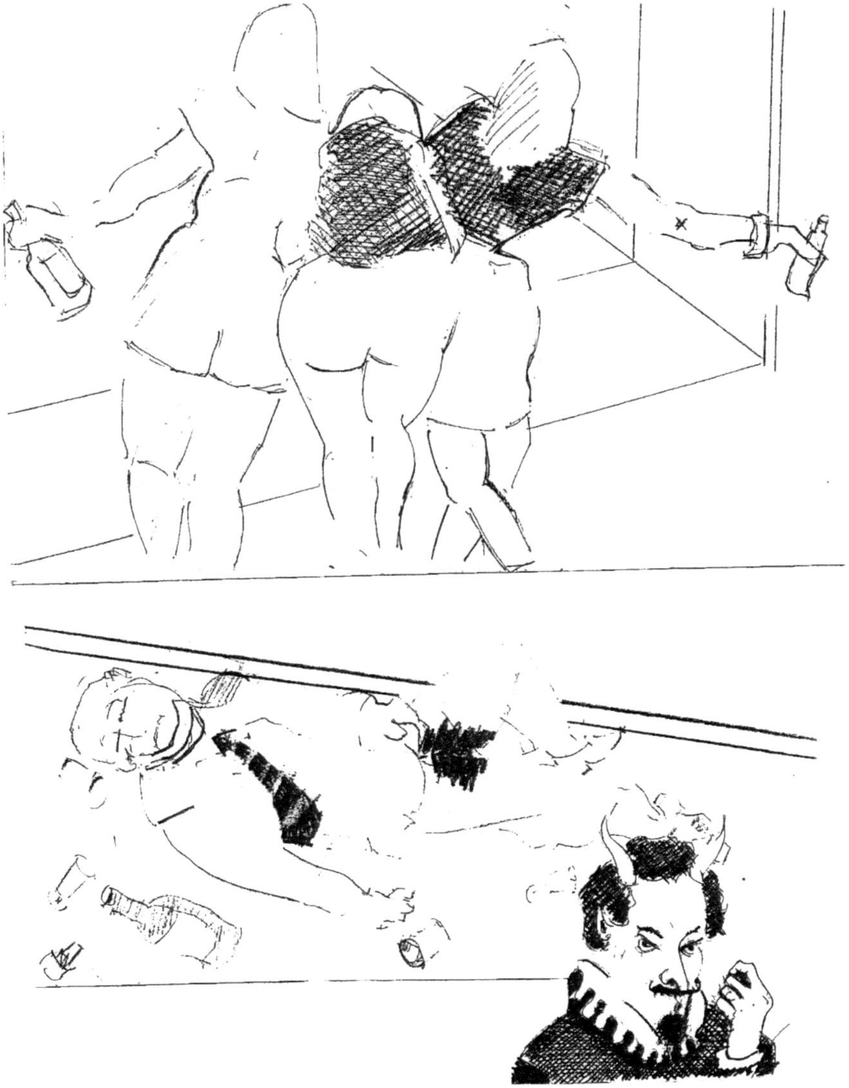

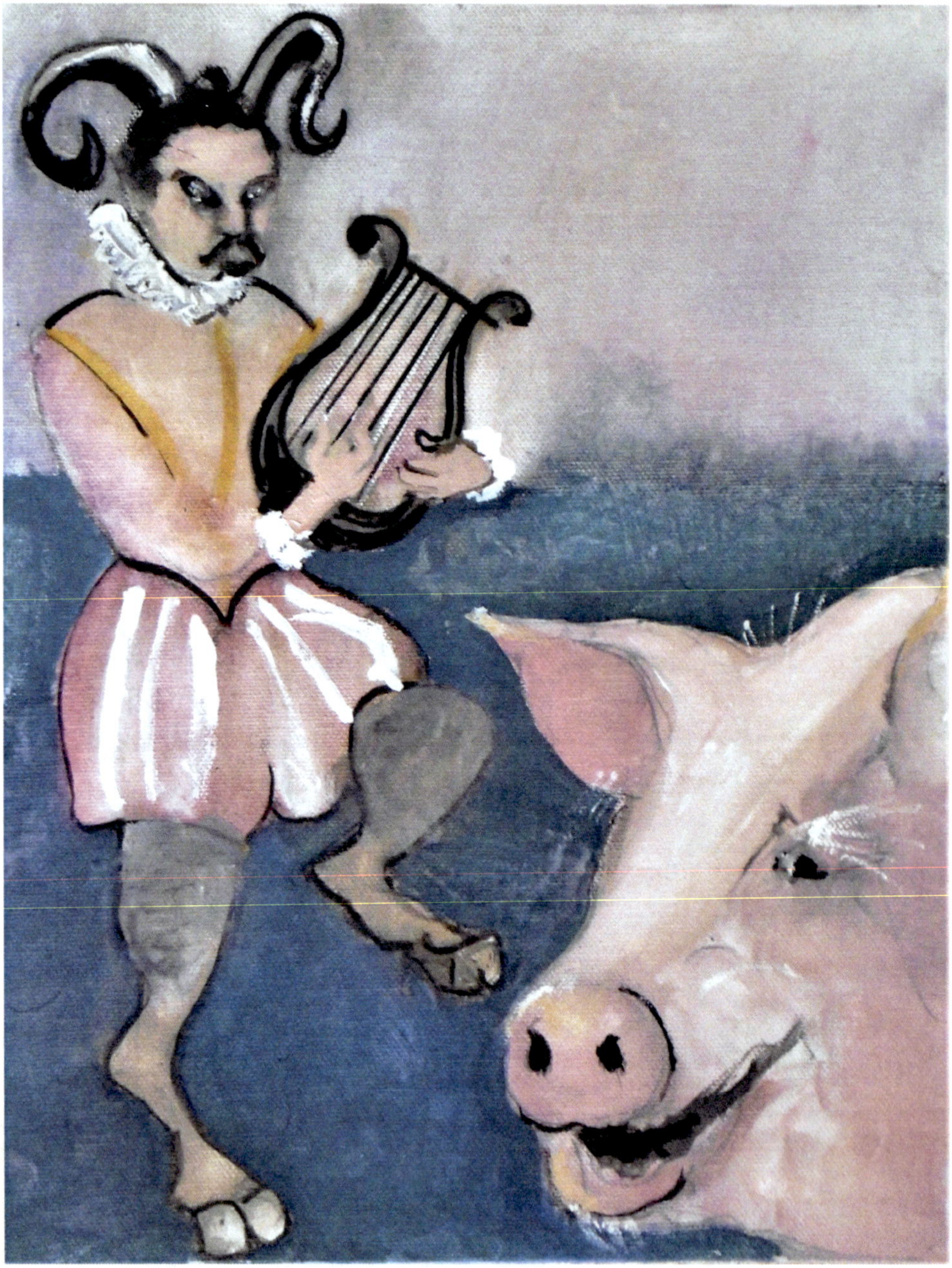

It's all tweet and defacebook, all troll and clinked in;
you've had your poke and it's time to defriend you.

But it seems my especial form of Damnation
is brief recurring reincarnation.
So, though I now slip through this virtual crack,
the chances are that I'll be back.

Fading…. Fading…. Over and out.

Over and out

        Transcript ends.